A PERSONAL QUEST THROUGH
QUESTIONS FOR

32 Questions

PARENTS, PROFESSIONALS,
AND BUSINESS TEAMS

Amy Hoppock

32 Questions: A Personal Quest through Questions for Parents,
Professionals, and Business Teams
By Amy Hoppock © 2017

Print ISBN: 978-1-61206-129-0
eBook ISBN: 978-1-61206-130-6

Production Team: Maryanna Young, Jennifer Regner, and Fusion
Creative Works

For more information on how to purchase this book at quantity dis-
counts email alohapublishing@gmail.com

To connect with the author, visit 32Questions.com

Published by

ALOHA
PUBLISHING

AlohaPublishing.com
First Printing
Printed in the United States of America

When you get your 'Who am I?' question right, all the 'What should I do?' questions tend to take care of themselves.

—Richard Rohr

The Akiva Questions

A story is often told of a Rabbi named Akiva who, while walking home one evening, was so intently lost in thought that he missed the corner in the road that led to his home. He continued to walk on, lost in deep thought, when suddenly out of the darkness a voice boomed, "Who are you and what are you here for?" Startled, Rabbi Akiva looked up and realized he was at the gate of a neighboring Roman city. Akiva responded, "How much are you paid to ask those questions?" The guard, puzzled by such an uncommon response said, "Five denarri a week." Akiva replied, "I'll pay you double that to come to my house and ask me those two questions at the start of every day."

Questions have power. Sometimes the simplest questions are the most profound.

You can answer the questions that follow daily for a month, one month every quarter of the year, or every day. Find a set time in your day and ask yourself the following simple, yet profound questions. There is space for you to write one or two sentences in response for each question.

What you can expect . . .

*Every day, as you think about the "Akiva questions," your answer may change, shift, and clarify as you come back to "Who am I?" and "What am I here for?"

*You will "know what you know." Many wise people tell us "our heart knows the way," and to "trust our instincts," "listen to your heart," or "you know what to do." It's true, you do, but figuring out how to "know what you know" isn't as easy as it sounds. These simple, profound questions can help you begin.

Getting Started

When will you answer your questions? (Finding a consistent time daily is best!)

Is there someone else you can work through these questions with and check in daily or once a week, to share the things you've learned?

Grab your book, a pencil, and get started!

Remember:

*There are no right or wrong answers.

*This is just for you—be honest. Honest answers are far more helpful than answers that sound good but don't reflect your heart.

One more thing . . .

Think about the "voice" that is asking the questions.

Is it a judgmental, critical voice?

Or, is it a kind, curious voice?

Both voices live with us. Let your kind, *curious*, thoughtful voice be the one asking the questions. These questions aren't about adding more fuel to the fire that your critical, judgmental voice may already be trying to stir up.

Stay Curious!! Be Kind!!

We listen for guidance everywhere

except from within.

—Parker Palmer

One life on this earth is all that we get,
whether it is enough or not enough, and
the obvious conclusion would seem to be
that at the very least we are fools if we do
not live it as fully and bravely
and beautifully as we can.

—Frederick Buechner

When we have a clear picture about our
own capacity, we can be realistic about our
effort. Then there is a much greater chance
of achieving our goals. But unrealistic effort
only brings disaster. So in many cases our
stress is caused by our expectations
and our ambition.

—the Dalai Lama

1

Who am I?

What am I here for?

What does my ideal day, week, and year look like?

2

Who am I?

What am I here for?

Have I stopped doing something I used to really enjoy and need to start doing it again?

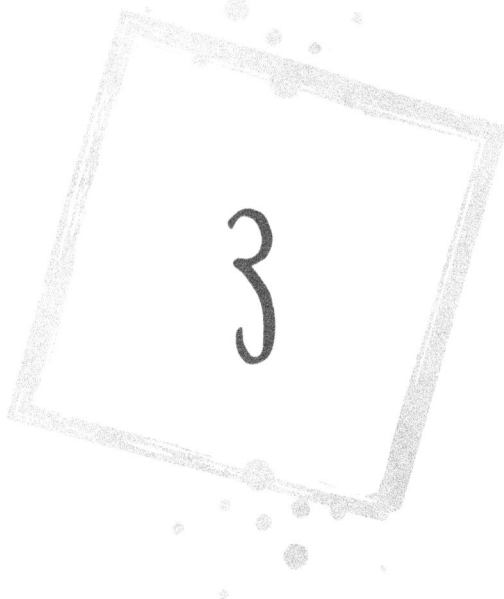

3

Who am I?

What am I here for?

How and where am I blocking my own success and
forward momentum?

4

Who am I?

What am I here for?

How can I plan my day/life around what I truly value?

5

Who am I?

What am I here for?

What is my heart telling me that I need to listen to?

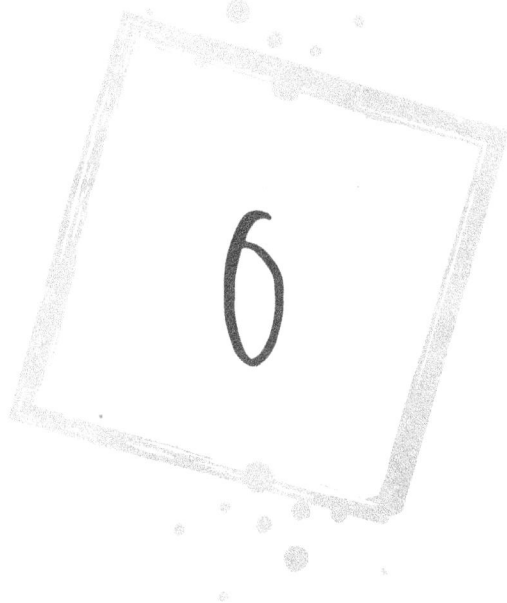

6

Who am I?

What am I here for?

Where can I add a new habit or positive pattern into my life?

7

Who am I?

What am I here for?

What are my personal blind spots that I have been unwilling to look at?

"Heart" comes from the Latin *cor* and points not merely to our emotions but to the core of the self, that center place where all of our ways of knowing converge—intellectual, emotional, sensory, intuitive, imaginative, experiential, relational, and bodily, among others.

The heart is where we integrate what we know in our minds with what we know in our bones, the place where our knowledge can become more fully human.

Cor is also the Latin root from which we get the word *courage*. When all that we understand of self and world comes together in the center place called the heart, we are more likely to find the courage to act humanely on what we know.

—Parker Palmer

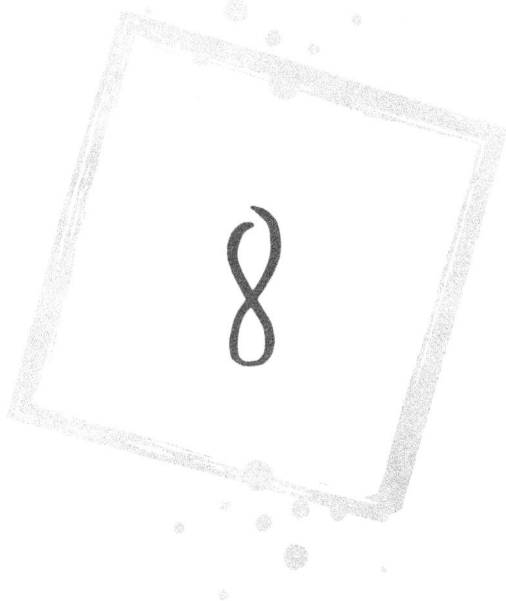

8

Who am I?

What am I here for?

Where am I letting fear have too much control over the choices that I make?

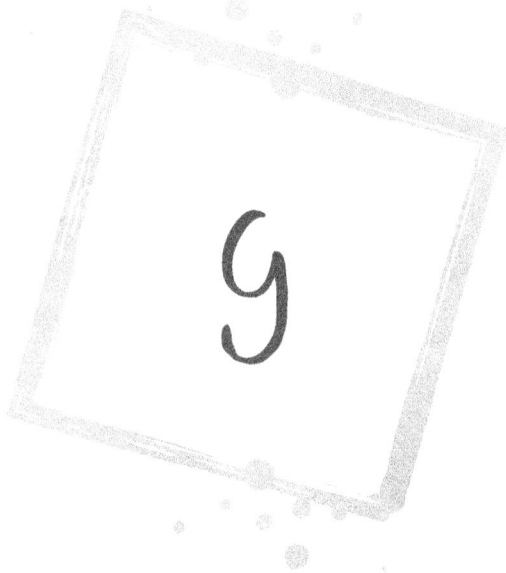

9

Who am I?

What am I here for?

Is there a place in my life that I need to ask for help
and let someone else in?

10

Who am I?

What am I here for?

What does leadership mean to me and where can I expand my leadership role?

11

Who am I?

What am I here for?

Where have I been giving others' expectations too much weight in my own decision-making?

12

Who am I?

What am I here for?

What lessons am I learning right now?

13

Who am I?

What am I here for?

Where do I need to own my part in a situation or life event, in order to forgive and move forward?

14

Who am I?

What am I here for?

What do I need to remove from my life? (Maybe an activity, commitment, or person.)

If success is not on your terms, if it looks good to the world but does not feel good in your own heart, it is no success at all.

—Anna Quindlen

15

Who am I?

What am I here for?

What one or two things do I need to do well? What must I stop doing, to do those things well?

16

Who am I?

What am I here for?

Where in my life do I have a belief that there isn't enough (success, opportunity, resources, etc.), which has stopped me from doing something I want to do?

17

Who am I?

What am I here for?

What is one thing I do really well?

18

Who am I?

What am I here for?

What stories am I telling myself that are holding me back?

19

Who am I?

What am I here for?

How do I face change?

20

Who am I?

What am I here for?

What long-term success am I working to create?

21

Who am I?

What am I here for?

Is there a place or situation in my life that I have been "playing it safe" out of fear?

May your choices reflect your hopes,

not your fears.

—Nelson Mandela

22

Who am I?

What am I here for?

Who needs to have *less* impact in my life?

23

Who am I?

What am I here for?

Who should I choose or allow to have *more* impact on my life?

24

Who am I?

What am I here for?

How am I making the changes I know are critical for my future?

25

Who am I?

What am I here for?

What brings me joy?

26

Who am I?

What am I here for?

What patterns do I keep repeating in my life and what can I learn from them?

27

Who am I?

What am I here for?

What skills do I have that others need and I am passionate about providing?

28

Who am I?

What am I here for?

What do I really want?

29

Who am I?

What am I here for?

What people in my life could help me achieve my goals?

30

Who am I?

What am I here for?

What is my biggest dream?

So what? Now what?

Questions are alive.

Questions echo.

Questions land in our head and rattle around, begging for attention and for us to engage and go on the *Quest* they are calling us to.

May the quest you have started with these questions be just the beginning of your next steps of brilliance and greatness.

The important thing is to not stop questioning.

—Albert Einstein

Resources

Books

Books open up new worlds, questions, and ideas. These are just a few great ones. Just as with asking yourself questions, be a curious reader. Read with a pen, ask questions of yourself and your assumptions. Read one book this year that challenges your assumptions or beliefs!

The Power of Now: A Guide to Spiritual Enlightenment by Eckhart Tolle
(Vancouver, B.C.: Namaste Publishing, 2004).

Body of Work: Finding the Thread That Ties Your Story Together by Pamela Slim
(New York: Portfolio/Penguin, 2013).

Everything Belongs: The Gift of Contemplative Prayer by Richard Rohr (New York: The Crossroad Publishing Company, revised and updated edition, 2003).

The Happiness Hypothesis: Finding Modern Truth in Ancient Wisdom by Jonathan Haidt
(New York: Basic Books, 2006).

Better Human: It's a Full-Time Job by Ronda Conger
(Boise: Elevate Publishing, 2016).

Podcasts

Podcasts are a great way to learn something new and engage with interesting and thought-provoking stories and ideas. A few great podcasts are:

This American Life
https://www.thisamericanlife.org/podcast

The Robcast
https://robbell.podbean.com/

Freakonomics
http://freakonomics.com/

Harry Potter and the Sacred Text
http://www.harrypottersacredtext.com/listen/

Building a Story Brand
http://buildingastorybrand.com/

And the possibilities are endless!

Find several that you love and listen for the questions. Be a curious and active listener.

Acknowledgments

Many thanks to Maryanna Young, Jennifer Regner,
Fusion Creative Works, and the Aloha Publishing
team that LIVES Aloha

To all the "question askers" in my life:

Jack and Cindy Varin—who always ask and never tell

Todd, Reid, and Delana—my greatest teachers

My Personal Notes

95

About the Author

Amy Hoppock is a questions collector and asker who lives in Boise, Idaho, with her family: Todd, Reid, and Delana. She believes in active listening and empowering people through the practice of asking questions.

Connect

For more questions and reflections, visit
32Questions.com

amy@32questions.com
#32questions
Instagram: 32 Questions

I am not afraid; I was born to do this.

—Joan of Arc

www.ingramcontent.com/pod-product-compliance
Lightning Source LLC
Chambersburg PA
CBHW070941210326
41520CB00021B/6994